THE LEADER'S ANCHOR

A TOOL TO FINDING EXPRESSION IN LEADERSHIP...

IMPACTOR VICTOR ELENDU

THE LEADER'S ANCHOR

PREFACE

This book summarizes key leadership qualities that are vital tools for everyone who wants to discover and actualize their desire to become top quality leaders in their areas of interest, calling or assignment. This is a study guide for all Christian leaders, especially, those who have successfully completed the evangelistic, discipleship and membership stages of their programmes.

This book will also be of immense value and relevance for individuals who are functioning as leaders in their various ministries, churches/fellowships. Also, the book is documented in a clear and simple style; and it is very useful, informative and educative.

CHAPTER ONE

NUGGET OF LEADERSHIP

Leadership is a position of authority, power and influence. Leadership can also be seen as a vehicle through which plans and actions are conceived, hatched and implemented. In other words, leadership is an effective means of getting things done or achieved through people and the proper management of money and resources. Dr. Myles Munroe called leadership a trusted privilege given by people to someone they want as their head. Leadership is the act of influencing, inspiring and motivating a group of people to achieve a desired goal.

Leadership is the ability to influence, inspire, or motivate men to join in the pursuit of a common goal and contribute towards its realization.

Good leadership in any organization, ministry churches/fellowship, country or society must be able to give proper direction and also point the way forward. Good leadership should be able to inspire confidence, faith and trust in people, who are the beneficiaries/the led.

Leadership in the Church/Fellowship, Family and Society:

Leadership is one of the basic pillars of progress and cohesion in any organization, family, church/fellowship or society. If the position of Leadership is not in place in any setting, the resultant effect and consequence is complete mayhem, confusion and chaos!

There was a time in the nation of Israel when things were bad and the people took "Laws" in their own hands and were doing things that fancied them. The Bible recorded for posterity thus;

> ***"In those days there was no king in Israel, but every man did that which was right in his own eyes"*** (Judges 17:6)

A society, country, churches or fellowship; that fails to provide good Leadership is also asking for trouble. In different parts of the world, including Africa, some countries have gone to war and broken-up because of bad leadership. People usually become restless, and demand for a change, restructuring, reformation, often times, becoming violent and out of control as a result of bad leadership.

Good leadership will inspire the people and the society at large towards progress and development.

A family that fails to give its members, good leadership is actually courting/causing trouble. The absence of good leadership in a family, especially, that of parents and guardians reflects in the bad morals and delinquencies usually displayed by children in these dys-functional families.

Leadership is also an essential factor in the fellowship/church. The Lord Jesus Christ succeeded in His earthly ministry because of His exemplary Leadership to His disciples and the people who benefited from His ministry.

The fellowship or church is built and function on leadership. The fellowship/church is propelled through the inspiration and leadership of the Holy Spirit using human instrument to accomplish God's divine purpose and counsel for the human race.

"And he gave some, evangelists"... (Eph. 4:11-12)

BASIC PRINCIPLES FOR EFFECT-IVE AND EFFICIENT LEADERSHIP

Leadership is anchored on some basic fundamentals for effectiveness and efficiency. If they are not solidly in place or incorporated in any form of leadership, then, that leadership is tantamount to failure. Therefore, any good leadership should be based on these principles:

❖ Leadership must recognize and depend on the grace of God. "For by Grace are..." (Eph. 2:8-9)

❖ Leadership must recognize the infallibility of God's word. "All scripture is given by..." (2Tim. 3:16-17)

❖ Leadership must recognize the place of wisdom. "Wisdom is the principal thing..." (Prov. 4:7)

❖ Leadership must recognize the value of service. "Feed the flock of God which is among you..." (1Pet. 5:2-3)

> **"But Jesus called them unto him, and said, you know that the princes..."** (Matt. 20:25-27)

Are you called to a position of leadership? Now that you know God's perspective of leadership, how would you respond to this challenge and demand of leadership in your life? Leadership is about leading and achieving Positive results. What would you do to begin to use your leadership gift and potentials to build up other people in order for them to reach their own potentials?

LEADERSHIP LAWS
(Joshua 1:6-9)

The Bible is the greatest book of wisdom that exists throughout the universe because it contains laws that, if obeyed, have the efficiency or capacity to make someone wise. In it are leadership laws that guarantee success to anyone who will obey them. These laws have work for so many persons in the old and are still working till today; the reason is because their source is from the initiator of leadership (God) who created man in His own image and likeness with a command to dominate (Gen. 1:27-30)

<u>What are Laws?</u> The whole system of rules that everyone in a country or society must obey is known as a law. It is also the rules which control an organization or activity.

That scripture above implies that man was created by God to rule (that is Leadership) hence provided with laws that when fully followed will be successful.

The laws are as follows:

LAW 1

<u>The Law of Integrity</u>: This law is emphatically on how a leader should live his or her life in leadership world. It talks about a leader to be honest; and having a high standard of moral values and principle.

"...but let your yea be yea; and your nay, nay..." **(James 5:12).**

"The man of integrity walks securely..." (Prov. 10:9 NIV)

Great leaders have integrity. They are honest with themselves, and to others (the people they lead).

<u>LAW 2</u>

<u>The law of Personal Effectiveness</u>: Great leaders focus on leading themselves first. They discipline themselves. Discipline is a self-imposed standard and restriction motivated by a desire that is greater than the alternatives. It is self-policing and is rooted in self-control. "Self-control is the most powerful kind of control. It is the hardest to master but produce the greatest (not the weakest) and the best (not the less) results". Aristotle (the Greek Philosopher) said. "I count him braver who conquered himself than he who took a city; for the greatest battle is the battle over self". The wise man said **"He that has no rule over his own spirit is like a city that is broken down, and without walls"** (Prov. 25:28). Paul said also **"...keep under my body, and bring it into subjection..."** (1Cor. 9:27, KJV) Great leaders work to improve their strengths and reduce their weakness.

<u>LAW 3</u>

<u>The Law of Foresight</u>: Great leaders succeed by developing the ability to see the future through the help of God by praying and asking for him to see beyond. **"...for all the land which you see, to you will I give it to..."** (Gen. 13:15).

Succeeding leaders are seeing leaders who know (by seeing beyond) the needs of the people he is leading. He understand (by seeing beyond) how the people he is leading feels. He knows (by seeing beyond) what will become, what will befall and what will benefit the people he is leading before effecting change.

"Any leader that lack or disobey this law will always stand at-ease when he is supposed to forward-match"

Great leaders see when to pursue and conquer whereas the reverse is the case of a leader that disobey or lack this law.

David asked the Lord if he should go after the band of the raiders. (*1 Sam. 30:6-8*)

Great Leaders sees when the people they are leading is hungry and make provision on time to avert its danger. Great leaders are vision-inclined. They have the ability to see and know what God is saying about his people, what they should do to achieve God's purpose in their life. A true and great leader has the ability to think about or plan the future with great imagination and intelligence (Prov. 29:18).

Visionary leaders are great because they are open to new information from God who put them there and other source (like the one you are reading now), they have the ability to experiment what they see unlike things others overlook. They possess mental foresight and are highly sensitive.

> *"They have a clear mental picture of their vision*
> *in the mission as commissioned leaders".*

They are not distracted by external or internal problems, hence are concerned about taking the people they lead from where they are to where they are expected to be.

LAW 4

<u>The Law of Courage</u>: Great Leaders are courageous because it is a command, a law that must be inside you as a leader. "This is my command-be strong and courageous…" (Josh. 1:9). Great leaders take courage to do what they really need to do. They don't allow or welcome fear. "They don't see battles as their enemy hence they quit but see it as a phenomenon for which success and victory is given birth." I am not ignorant of the fact that a lot of people in leadership are fear stricken because of lack of courage; they have the fear of (F-3);

1.   **Faces**: The fear of faces is the fear of people. It's the fear of what people will say, what people will think. "No one can make you feel inferior without your consent" says Jentezen Franklin (a New York Time best-selling author of fasting). God told them including Joshua not to be afraid of their faces.

2.   **Fences**: This is the fear of barriers, and road-blocks/stumbling blocks. We're afraid that it will be too hard or high. It might hurt. Charles Lindbergh said, "Success is not measured by what a man accomplishes, but by the opposition he encountered and the courage he maintained in his struggle against it".

3.   **Failure**: They always cover up and say isn't that what really stops us every time? We like all like the idea of success but overlook the process that gave birth to that success we cherish so soon. We like to win but give less attention on the process that birthed the winning (victory). It's the "what ifs" that get us. "What if I make a fool of myself? What if… what if… and the next thing you know, you're back in your easy

going lifestyle of leadership, you are back in your easy chair, not going anywhere, not doing anything. A true and great leader who is courageous will always say yes if... to any what if's... that may arise as a leader in the midst of fear. Fear of course because anybody who ever beat the odds or make a difference in leadership did it in spite of their fear. What are you waiting for, a feeling of courage? Forget it! It doesn't exist; you're only courageous when you do what's right despite your fears. The courage David had to fight Goliath made him automatically a leader.

As a leader in any leadership setting you found yourself, make the decision today to obey these laws if you want progress in your reign and if something is wrong with your leadership, don't blame your people. Instead look out for what is missing in your leadership and add. If you lack any of this laws in you as a leader in your family, fellowship/church etc, don't blame any of your member rather look out for what is missing in your leadership as you apply them and add, you will live a fulfilled person.

LEADERSHIP LEVELS

Have you ever asked yourself why we don't add any title to the name of Jesus? Or address Him with those big titles? We just call Him Jesus and He answers us. Unlike our time leaders that buy titles and carry it as if it really count. In fact, never you make mistake not addressing them with their titles that due them and you will regret to see their next reaction. I'm not against according someone with titles that due him/ her but let me also say that those titles does not add to whatever you're not capable of doing as a leader.

We don't call Jesus Archbishop Jesus, Vicar Jesus, Most Rev'd Jesus, Pope Jesus, and Most exalted President Jesus, Pastor Jesus and so on. It is because He operated at a distinct level of leadership. His name alone compels every force and protocol to bow. Phil. 2:5-11 **"...at the name of Jesus every knee should bow..."**

Leadership exists in different levels which are:

➢ **Positional Leadership**: (your boss chooses you to hold a position).

➢ **Permission Leadership**: (people allow you to lead them).

➢ **Production leadership**: (you are respected to producing superior results).

➢ **People-Development Leadership**: (people follow you because of what you have done for them).

➢ **Personhood Leadership**: This is the highest level

of leadership. Jesus Christ is our perfect example here. His name alone commands honour, respect, dignity and glory. If you care to know, even the whole world needs He's name to have peace. People call His name when there is emergency, when an accident is about to occur or when there is killings here and there. Even the unbelievers call His name too.

But remember that He paid the needed price before he got that name. What price are you also willing to pay so that you can also operate at the personhood level of leadership? You are surprised? Yes, you can also operate there. It was not only Jesus that operated at that level of leadership; He also had sons and daughters who operate at the personhood level of leadership. Mother Theresa; Smith Wigglesworth, Reinhard Bonnke, Abraham the father of faith and many more, all operated at that level of leadership. Nobody has to add a title to their names; their name already is a title. At the personhood level of leadership, people follow you because of your success in leadership. They follow you because of who you are, whom you have become and what you represent. This level of leadership is reserved for leaders who have spent years growing people and organizations. You can pay the price. But you have better start now if you have not started at all and you have to make a decision to continue if you have already started. Make a decision today to move up on your leadership level or cadre. If the only thing that gives you respect as a leader is your position, you have already failed because positional leadership is the lowest level of leadership.

➢   **The Eagle leadership**: The eagle is unique in every way to other birds. It has unique qualities that make it unique, distinct and even different from other birds. The following are some of the abilities/qualities:

❖ **It Has the Power of Vision**: It can see very far. It has the ability to see or detect any coming challenge before it get to it. As earlier said that as a leader or true and great leader you must possess this ability.

❖ **It Develops Ability to Carry a Weight that is Three time its Size**: This implies that it is not a weak bird. It excels in strength. This is courage in application and action.

❖ **It is Swift**: Its movement is not slow at all. It moves very fast to catch its preys or to do what it has to do.

❖ **It Patiently Waits for the Appropriate Wind and Soars on it**: When other birds are struggling to fly, the eagle soars on the wind. It goes to the highest branch of a very tall tree and patiently waits for the wind. When it senses it, it moves and soars on the wind. Soaring means effortless flying. The wind carries the eagle to the destination the eagle desires to go. As a leader, you should have the ability to wait, endure/patiently wait on the Lord and hear what He intends to say on that issue before making move. That makes you an eagle leader.

> *"...they shall mount up with wings as eagles..."*
> (Isaiah 40:30-31)

<u>Like an Eagle, you must see Farther</u>: Isaiah 40:30-31,

> *"...the eyes of your understanding being enlightened..."*
> (Eph. 1:16-19)

Like an eagle, a true and great leader must see farther than his other team members. In fact, this is what will make his team members respect his leadership. If the only thing that his followers are seeing is what he also is seeing, he will begin to lose his credibility to lead them gradually. This is because there is no point following a leader that you cannot learn from. Some people will agree to follow your leadership because they are interested in your vision even before they get to know you deeply. The first hand disciples of our Lord Jesus Christ first got attracted to the vision that He came to them with before they actually knew Him. This is applicable to family leaders and the society at large. In fact that is why circular leadership requires that you campaign, convince and inspire the audience/wife to be with a clearly stated vision to vote/marry you. As a great leader, you should meditate on a new thing you can introduce to your team.

Like an eagle; you must be Stronger:

"...I can do all things through Christ..." (Philippians 4:13). At one time, it was recorded that a president of the U.S.A only has two hours in a day to sleep. How about that, other hours are for various kinds of meetings that have already been scheduled for him that he must attend. Like an eagle, a great leader must develop his physical ability. One major area to prepare for before stepping into leadership is the development of one's physical ability. Start stretching yourself now. Go the extra mile in your daily work input. Increase your work inclination. It will be hard to be effective in leadership if you are weak in your body. Stress yourself now, so that issues in leadership (both the family, circular leadership) will not stress you up later. For how many hours can you fast and pray in a day? For how long can you sit and stay awake in study? Do you easily get tired of issues or you like to brainstorm for ways of escape? Think on these things. In Isaiah 54:4, God says **"...Lengthen your cords..."** it also implies that you develop your physical ability to function longer under stress. Do something extra today.

<u>Like an eagle, you must be Swift:</u>

Like an eagle, a true and great leader must be swift in making great decision that can help the team and the people he/she is leading. The Bible Book of Deut. 30:19 put it "...therefore choose life..." one of the most frustrating things in leadership of all setting is to have a leader who is very slow in making the right decision. It is decisions that either make you or mar you as a leader. Great decisions make great leaders and bad decisions mar/make bad leaders. Life itself is a cycle of decisions for we cannot do without making decision daily. You're going out, standing up from your bed side after you wake up in the morning is decision. In fact, not making any move at all, not making decisions, itself is a decision. Life is a choice, so also is success (good) and failure (bad) a choice between life and death, between blessings and curses. Now..." (Deut. 30:19), beloved, it is a matter of now. In fact, reluctance in making and taking decisions that will help the team and the led is one characteristic of weak leaders. Some leaders don't want to take quick decisions, not because they are waiting for an appropriate time but because they are afraid or they are trying to be perfect (they don't want to make any mistake). However, when the followers (the led) or team members discover this, the trust they have for that leader begins to die gradually.

When a man refuses to take decisions on important issues in the family, even when it is clear to the wife that the husband ought to have done this for the family, the wife's trust for her husband gradually begins to die. That alone can signal unforeseen danger in the family.

As a true and great leader, don't be slow in making and talking decisions that will help your team and followers become better and greater. If you don't make or take that decisions and they see another leader making or taking that decisions, they will leave your leadership and follow the other leader that meet and suit their needs and lifestyle. Don't postpone that decision that will help them and help you, take it now. **"...come now let's..."** (Isaiah 1:18). I pray that the Lord God will lead you in the way you should go.

Like an eagle, you must be Sensitive:

Like an eagle, a true and great leader must be sensitive to the right timing before taking an action.

"A good act at a wrong time becomes a wrong act altogether"

The wise king in his book according to Ecclesiastes 3:1 which is a great Biblical article on time. The summary of that great article is *"...there is time for everything and a purpose for everything..."* (Ecclesiastes 3:1)

Hence, wisdom demands that before a leader decides to take an action, he must first understand what the time, the period, the circumstance, is saying directly or indirectly. Some corrections can be taken for abuse if they are given at the wrong time. One great quality that made the children of Issachar stand out among other Israeli was the fact that they had the understanding of the times and knew what the entire nation of Israel should be involved in at a particular time according to 1 Chronicles 12:32. Among the thousands of warriors who joined David's Army, 200 were outstanding not only were they warriors, they were leaders with understanding of the times and knew the best course for Israel to take.

Just like the Eagle waits for the right time and the right wind before it moves, a great leader must wait for the right time before taking the right actions. As a great leader, you need to gather all the necessary information needed before taking that step, may the Lord baptize you with the spirit of patience and discernment of spirit. Amen.

THE WASTEFUL LEADERSHIP:

"...and the philistine slew Jonathan..." (I Samuel 31:2).

Time is life! Life, itself, can be broken down into capsule of time. Time is one great gift that God had given to us to profit withal. And anything that wastes your time automatically wastes your life. One of those thing that waste your time is; staying under a wasteful Leadership of any setting.

Any Leadership you stay or operate under that does not contribute to your progress in life is wasting your time indirectly. Any leadership (churches, fellowship, family, company etc) that does not help or contribute to the execution of God's plans for your life is also a wasteful leadership. Be wise! Don't be emotional about it. That was the mistake of Jonathan, the son of King Saul. Jonathan knew God had taken away the kingdom from his father, King Saul, and had given it to David his friend, who was also a servant under Saul, yet Jonathan continued to follow Saul until he lost his life. He was emotional about leaving his father. You may be disturbed with the quest in your heart; if you're to leave your father/your husband after considering the fact that your father will always remain your father, and that your marriage oat is for better and for worse. No! Don't break up with them but also don't follow them in their act, in their leadership. You don't have a spare life! You better use this one that you have well. Cut off from any association, company, and church/fellowship that waste your life today. Always ask yourself if your life has been better since you started following that man / woman? May God help you to dissociate yourself from the wrong association today? In Jesus Name, Amen!

THE BALANCE LEADERSHIP:

Leadership exists in different categories and is expressed in different ways. It's not only about service; leadership also means influence. Several positional leaders as earlier mentioned have complained that they have done everything possible to win the heart of the people they lead, they have served them to the best of their knowledge yet the people are not yielding correctly to their leadership. In one of the leadership setting which l happen to be a team member, during my leadership up bringing; l noticed that the leaders in the team had issues of not yielding to the overall leader's leadership, almost all the time with almost half of the team members. This made him quarrel on different occasions with them, all because he lacks influence, I mean, positive influence. If not by some selected few of this leaders in the team who took it upon themselves to pray over it and by the special grace of God, he would have destroyed his service at the peak of him saying, I have finish the course, l have kept the faith. "Leadership that operates only on the level of service and not influence is an incomplete leadership" let us look at the meaning of leadership; "the ability to influence, inspire, or motivate men to join in the pursuit of a common goal and contribute towards its realization. Now get this right that influence here is not to control or manipulation of others, it is not by making the people you lead to go through pain. It is not by having Lord over them in all. For instance; it must be what you think, want or say, that must stand and nothing more. "It is not how hard you raise your voice, raise your hand, press on them but how high and deep you have positively influence them that matter most". True leadership especially in the Christian setting, is not manipulation or suppression of others; rather it is a wilful submission of others authority to the leader's authority. A true leader therefore, obtains the follower's submission or compliance without their resistance (not in spite of their resistance). The influence is not through deceit or the use of threat and violence. Such is better called manipulation, oppression or dictatorship.

So, service makes people love your leadership but positive influence makes people respect your leadership. Service can make people get interested in your leadership but positive influence will make people commit to your leadership. Which of these would you choose to follow or get committed to; the man that gives you fish everyday or the man that teaches you how to catch fish? The former is likened to a leader that renders service without influence whereas the later is likened to a leader that influences with his services. Are you living a balanced leadership life? If no is the answer' lunch out today in your leadership life to influence (impact positively) on your followers (led) and you will be glad you did.

CHAPTER TWO

CONCEPTUAL MODEL OF A LEADER

In Africa, a leader is an individual, usually a male person who wields much influence and commands the respect of other people, because of the power and constituted authority associated with his position in the community or society.

The word "LEADER" is not a label or title you give yourself but what the people whom you inspire (lead) followers, call you because they are stirred to participate in the pursuit of the vision you presented to them. Traditional chiefs; like Emir, Obas, Obis, etc. Also Religious leaders Like Pope, Bishops, Rev'rds, Pastors, Evangelist etc, are all examples of leaders who are held in high esteem and honour by virtue of their Position in the community or society and their calling from God to benefit human race. They are revered and their pronouncements are regarded and treated with importance and sometimes seen as laws, which no one dares to disregard or disobey.

In ancient Israel, the Bible recorded for prosperity exploits of people who were chosen as leaders by God for specific functions and purposes in the nation of Israel. Abraham, Moses, Joshua, David, only to mention but a few; were chosen by God to carry out different functions and assignments in their own time and generation in Israel. Today, we have people who have been chosen, elected or appointed, as leaders to carry out specific functions and duties. Presidents, Governors, Chairmen etc, are typical leaders who have been appointed or elected by their countrymen and women for the purpose of smooth running of machineries of governance. Leaders are made from problem-solving, that's why problem-solving is the shortest route to leadership. It is the ability of an individual to solve a problem and gain mastery over the problem that determines whether the person will be a leader or not.

THE CALLING OF A LEADER:

A leader is known and distinguished from the crowd mainly through his responsibilities, duties, and functions as a result of the position he / she occupies in the community, society, country, church / fellowship etc. Moses is a very good example of a person who was distinguished, respected, revered and honoured, because of the exalted position of his calling among his people, the Israeli. Moses as a leader was called by God to lead the Israeli out of slavery and bondage in Egypt into freedom. He had a lot of problems, challenges, and situations that were too difficult for him to handle as a single individual. He faced oppositions from both his people (Israeli) and the Egyptians arch enemies of the Israeli. In Israel, Moses name is indelibly etched in history due to his accomplishments as a leader.

True and great leaders, like Moses are specifically called and given their assignments by God. Their missions are clearly defined; and such leaders because they have their mandates from God, objectively commit themselves towards the actualization of their God-given dreams and visions.

"...And when the Lord saw that he turned aside to see, God called him out of the midst of the bush, and said..."
(Exodus 3:4, 9-10).

Are you committed in the actualization of God given dreams, visions and purpose of your followers and yours? Then cheers because you are in the right track of leadership.

A LEADER AS A CATALYST OF DEVELOPMENT:

Solomon was the son of David. Like David his father, he was also a leader of the nation of Israel. He was a wise king. As a leader, he carried out his functions and assignment with wisdom. One of the assignments he executed was; the temple building project. The temple project was first of its kind in Israel. Solomon through his wisdom and God's guidance was able to gather enough resources and materials to accomplish the gigantic task of building a befitting temple for God. At the completion of temple, important dignitaries and visitors like the Queen of Sheba was attracted hence travelled from far their countries to see the beauty, glory and splendour of the temple. A true and great leader is a catalyst of development, change and good happenings. Through his exalted position in the society, a true leader is able to initiate and execute programmes and plans that will bring about change, development and progress to his followers in particular and the society in general. A true leader apart from being a catalyst of development and progress is also an instrument of great influence for his followers and other people in the society. The influence here is not by oppressing the people you're leading, is not by exposing them to hunger by removing food on their tables, which to make sure they eat, they become slaves in your hand, No! This is not influence, this is simply wickedness. The influence a true leader should exercise on his followers is what I call positive impact. The greatest test for a leader is his ability to reproduce himself in the lives of other people, for continuity of his visions and programmes.

THE CHRISTIAN LEADER:

This is an individual who understands the nature of his calling and fulfils his duties and responsibilities through his position as a leader in the church / fellowship.

The Christian leader is committed and dedicated to his vision and counsel of God for his life. Paul, while defending himself against his accusers, boldly affirmed that;

> *"...therefore, O king Agrippa, I was not disobedient unto the heavenly vision: but showed first unto them of Damascus, and..."* (Acts 26:19-20)

Thus, the Christian leader is a person who fears God: and who also recognizes that his position of Leadership comes from God, hence remains committed and dedicated to God and him alone. Are you a leader or serving under a leader? Whatever position or status that you occupy, you must recognize that you have been called by God to function effectively and efficiently in that capacity, not to lord it all over your follower by oppressing them both in your decisions (I mean a case where it must be your decisions that must count), definitely not so. I have served under leaders that after taking a conclusion in an official meeting still goes back to do what they intend doing even when the opinion was not seconded. That is not influence. That is oppression and dictatorship; which is not and must not be seen especially in a Christian leader.

No single individual or person is here on earth without a purpose. Everyone of us in life must find our niche and begin to do something worthwhile in life.

CHAPTER THREE

THE MAKING OF A LEADER:

In the previous chapters, we studied Nuggets of leadership, and conceptual model of a leader. To refresh our memories, we can go back to read these chapters. In this chapter the emphasis is on how to become a leader. In the Bible, we have record of leader's -men and women, who were called by God; and some who were elected by the people (e.g. Stephen). They all performed their roles as leaders to the best of their abilities. Some of these leaders were successful and outstanding in their own time, whereas some of them also failed in their capacities as leader. We shall discuss the reasons why some leaders fail in their roles, duties and responsibilities but this chapter is strictly on the making of a leader. In our society, we are very familiar with some people we hold in high esteem and respect because of their positions as leaders. How did these individuals become leaders? Did they become leaders from birth or Childhood? Were these men and women specially made, prepared, and entrusted into leadership position? Your ability to answer these questions will make you to be conscious that you're also a leader in the making by reading this piece of material.

The following are some of the factors that are responsible for an individual or person becoming a leader:

- **<u>By Calling</u>**: This is God, setting an individual apart for a divine assignment to accomplish a specific task in life and also it is one of the ways by which an individual can be called into leadership position, in his community or society.

There are several Biblical accounts of individuals, such as father Abraham, Moses, David, Jeremiah, etc who were leader in ancient Israel as a result of their calling by God. Prophet Jeremiah's call by God as a leader in Israel is very instructive:

> *"...Then the word of the LORD came unto me saying, before I formed you ..."* (Jer. 1:5)

I'm aware of the facts that some persons have all ruled it out that it no longer happens in our time, they even make mockery of you when you come up with such like one so-called man of God who have severally come out in public telling people that God said he should contest in the presidential position, that he is the next president, and he did contested in the election failing woefully. But in all of these it still exist, in fact, it is still happening. God is still raising prophets, leaders in our time. You may/can be the one.

- **<u>By Recognition of Gifts</u>**: Every individual has an appreciable deposit of gifts, talents and potentials to make him/her a great and respectable leader in his/her community, society, country, church/fellowship. It is the responsibility of every man and/or

woman to discover and pursue their areas of gifting in life. The word of God affirms thus:
"...A man's gifts make room for him, and brings..."
(Prov. 18:16).

Recognizing and pursuing your areas of greatest impact or gift makes you more responsible and valuable in your community, society, and church/fellowship. As a person or individual, what is that thing, gift, or act you're being noticed for that buy people's interest and at the same time gives you joy. What is that gift you're being highly recognized or figured out for whenever you are around people that make them follow you? I argue you to stand out with that gifting and you're a leader all the way.

- **By Apprenticeship/Training**: Potential leaders can, and, should undergo apprenticeship or training, which definitely enhance the qualities of their leadership inputs in whatever position or capacity they might occupy in their respective leadership setting to which is one of the basic aim of this piece of material.

Samuel was a great leader and prophet in ancient Israel. He was not just great he had his own share of service under another man of God called Eli. Elisha is another good example of a great leader who went through apprenticeship/training under the leadership of Prophet Elijah. Training is an essential ingredient, which an individual must be willing to undergo, in order to become a leader in any leadership setting in our Community or Society. Are you a leader by apprenticeship/training in your locality and you do not take it serious? You do not add value to it? Instead; you cover up with reasonable excuses you said; for a life time opportunity which may not appear or come again? There is this saying that "when the value of a thing is being lost, Abuse is inevitable. Are you reading it like ordinary book and planning to drop/throw it away after glancing through it. Also know that readers are leaders. Be wise and make good use of this one.

- **<u>By Service</u>:** An individual or person is entrusted into position of leadership either by calling, recognition of gifts, apprenticeship/training, or by service. Jephthah is a good example of an individual who become a leader as a result of his acceptance to render service to his people, the Israeli.

Jephthah rallied round his people in their time of need, and helped in defeating the enemies of the Israeli. He later became a leader among his people. Leadership is a sensitive and vital position in life. It is very intoxicating so be careful, hence you become a tyrant instead of a leader. Everyone of us have the potential to become a leader in his/her lifetime. This is the reason why I'm angry with those so called persons/individuals that shrink away from the leadership position given to them, with the excuses that they are not prepared for it. That they cannot handle it, that they don't have the abilities, qualities and so on... goodness to you, if you fall in any of these excuses because that is the main purpose of this book. We as an individual at all time must be ready to take responsibilities, one of such responsibilities is for you not to reject leadership because whether you like it or not, you're and will be a leader either by the above process. We must endeavour to stir up our gifts by developing our leadership potentials by reading materials like this because readers are leaders. The world is waiting for our emergence as leaders. Light dispels darkness. Knowledge puts to flight ignorance. You have a responsibility to discover who you are by discovering and putting into practice your gifts and potentials. Self-discovery is a step towards becoming a leader. Discover yourself today and lead in your place of position in Jesus Name Amen.

CHAPTER FOUR

GROOMING LEADERSHIP QUALITIES WITH CHARACTER

We have made justice in the previous chapter on Leadership, who a leader is and how to become a leader, but have not really said much on the qualities of a leader, hence this chapter. It is aimed at a leader grooming leadership qualities coupled with character, because in leadership character counts. Though; leadership is key in whatever thing we are doing. If you add leadership to whatsoever thing you are doing, it will grow farther, that is why even our life does not progress beyond the level we want it until we lead our lives which is character. In fact there is a saying that "if you want to test your leadership, look behind you, especially in time of trouble and difficulty, and see how many people that are still following you. This implies that it takes love and belief in a leader to follow him, let alone in time of trouble but what makes an individual to be so acceptable to his people even to the extent willing to submit to him and work towards the actualization of his vision? Character of course!

"When the righteous are in authority, the people rejoice,

but when the wicked man rules..." (Prov. 29:2).

What makes a leader good or bad is not in the office he occupies or the title he bears in him which implies his character. It is not in the position he occupies but in the disposition he portrayed. It is in his disposition of duties that will either make the people rejoice or groan. You either follow him or restrain from him. A true leader do not seek or run after his followers but attract them by his character. Character is attitude on display when one has his freedom. It is an expression of one's true self. Little wonder no individual can rise above his character.

The quality of a man's leadership is the result of his character. Leadership is not a pursuit but a result. Winston Churchill in his words said "Attitude" (character), "is a little thing that makes a big difference" it is in it that habits are formed, character developed, and a life is made or marred. Myles Munroe adduced that leadership, talent, skills and technical knowledge is 20% but attitudes (character) are 80%. It then implies that the acceptance or rejection of an individual's leadership depends on his character, character count because the effectiveness or ineffectiveness of a man's leadership is a product of his character, most often than not, on his character. The character of leaders can make or mar his administration, for your character determines what you administer. In fact, the striking and shocking problem rocking most countries, organization, parties, and even ministries today is leadership crisis. Little wonder questions of moral integrity, honour, values, role modelling, charisma, and respectable standards are well known topics on our daily news, programs and in the thought of the common man on the street. We see and hear of leaders involving in embezzlement of fund, sexual immorality, blatant hypocrisy, double standards, and inconsistencies, to mention but a few. Some even go to the extent of changing the existing laws/principles to suit their diabolic and selfish character. We also see and hear of abuse of authority and office, even among those in sacred establishment and commission. These days, the demand for a true leadership in our society is so high like never before. Leadership is critical to progress and if you desire it, take note of the following qualities of great leaders:

<u>VISION:</u>

Vision is an essential quality that a leader must possess. Good and successful leaders are visionaries. They have the ability to "Catch" a vision and to "Cast" this vision to their followers. It is not only the ability to receive, see, or catch a vision that makes an individual or person a great, true and successful leader but the ability to be able to project, cast, or sell this vision for acceptability to the people (followers) that makes such a person a very successful leader. Vision, hence, is an essential ingredient for success in leadership.

<u>CONCEPT OF VISION:</u>

The reality of our present times is the painful realization that some individuals who have been placed into trusted position (leadership) do not even have visible programmes, plans or ideas, which they have strategically mapped out or outlined for the people they are supposed to be directing or leading. A leader must have a clear vision for the people he/she is leading.

"...And the lord answered me and said; write the

vision and make it plain..." (Habkk. 2:2).

A leader must, because it is a command from God Himself, write the vision and make it plain to his/her followers.

"...I will come to visions and revelations of the Lord..."
(2Cor. 12:1).

Even Paul, the New Testament leader has to come to visions. You may not have the same vision as Paul, but you too will come to the particular vision that is the will of God for your life and that of your followers; those things that God wants you to accomplish. You need to recognise them as being yours from the Lord. Vision, therefore is having a purposeful and strategic initiation of ideas, plans and programmes, carefully drawn out by a leader with the main aim of implementing or executing such for the people or followers.

A vision is farther different from goal setting. There is nothing wrong with having goals, but a vision is not the same thing with goal setting. You set up a goal with your mental or carnal human mind. A vision originates from God. It is a spiritual thing. God puts it in your spirit. It will always be bigger than what you thought you could ever do or be, though impossible to achieve without the continual help of the Holy Spirit. The scripture affirms that:

"...where there is no vision, the people perish..." (Prov. 29:18)

Vision separates quack and deceitful leaders from real and trustworthy leaders.

Five things vision does for a leader:

1. Vision Motivates a leader
2. Vision gives Direction to a leader
3. Vision gives Stability to a leader

4. Vision brings Loyalty to a leader from his or her followers.
5. Vision acts as a Catalyst or Springboard for development.

Moses was a very strong, successful and charismatic leader. God gave Moses a vision to lead the Israeli out of bondage in Egypt. Moses received his mandate from God; but it was his duty to convince his people, the Israelite to receive the vision of being set free from bondage in Egypt.

Vision shows perceptibility and visibility. A leader must have this quality; it is very essential. The follower of a leader is bound to suffer if the leader does not have a clear visible plan of action or workable vision. The word of God says *"...where there is no vision, the people perish..."* (Prov. 29:18). The lack of vision is a miss-direction of focus. Vision ensures that the leaders mind is firmly fixed on its main goal or objective. Vision motivates, and also gives direction to a leader. It brings about stability. In whatever capacity you may presently occupy as a leader, you need a plan of action or vision to keep you going stronger in the direction. As a leader, you must keep your vision before you. A leader's vision is his road map to success. As a true leader, do you have a vision; a clear vision in that matter?

DILIGENCE:

Success in life, ministry, work or business, etc, requires a great application of diligence. There is no worthwhile achievement that has ever been accomplished in history, since the emergence of man on earth that has not been as a result of calculated hard work or diligence. Diligence is a steady, carefully, relentless effort in getting a job done; or the actualization of a dream, vision or project. Diligence is an essential ingredient of result-oriented leadership. The individual, who is a leader, and lacks diligence, will definitely not go too far before the weight of his laxity and slothfulness overwhelms him. The demands and responsibilities of leadership are not for the slothful; it is only for the very resourceful and diligent person. Apostle Paul, while, entrusting some leadership duties and responsibilities on his young protégé, Timothy, advised him to be very consistent and diligent.

> *"...Be diligent in these matters; so that everyone may see your progress..."* (1 Tim. 4:15 NIV)

As a true leader, you must be up and doing else you will crash over night in your leadership. As a leader, you must start winning from within you before you can win from outside you.

> *"...Keep thy heart with all diligence; for out of it are the issues of life..."* (Prov. 4:23).

So you can see that your heart needs to be diligent to withstand the battles that are going on in it. For in it are issues; tough, serious, shocking, and striking issues of life. And it is only the diligent that prevails. May I shock you with these; that the heart of man is always at work, the heart do not sleep. It is always awake. Little wonder the wise man said we should guard our heart above all else. This implies being steadfast, careful and relentless about how we discharges our duties as leaders.

WHY DILIGENCE? We cannot overemphasize the need for diligence in whatever assignment or work we have been asked to do as workers or leaders in our respective calling or vocations.

The leader who is very diligent in his work or assignment would inspire confidence and ignite the flame of enthusiasm in his followers or the led. When the people know that the leader is effective and result oriented because of his positive attitude and commitment to his assignment, duty or work, they would be encourage to put up the same attitude to work. The leader who is very diligent in his work will achieve more success and make progress than another individual who is also a leader but not too committed and dedicated to his assignment or calling.

> *"...See you a man diligent in his business?*
> *He shall stand..."* (Prov. 22:9).

The Lord God attaches much value and importance to leadership. The reason is not far-fetched. Leadership is God's service, either in a Church/fellowship or ministry plays a vital role in instructing and moulding the lives of men and women after the divine counsel of God.

> *"...But, beloved, we are persuaded better things*
> *of you, and things that accompany salvation,*
> *through we thus speak..."* (Hebr. 6:9-11).

Fruitfulness in ministry is greatly anchored on diligence. Apostle Paul was highly successful in his ministry because, he was a diligent worker. Brother Paul never took the grace of God on his life for granted. He never slacked, or become discouraged in the face of severe testing, trails and oppositions that confronted him. In the midst of confrontation with his opponents, sometimes at the risk of his life, Paul, never looked back but always trusted on God who had called him. Paul's diligent pursuit enabled him to accomplish all that was committed into his hands. Diligence will always produce positive result for a leader who is committed to his/her work, calling or assignment.

> *"...He becomes poor who has a slack hand but the hand of the diligent makes rich..."* (Prov. 10:4).

Diligence is the opposite of slothfulness: a leader who wants to succeed in his calling, assignment and mission must be an unrepentant diligent individual. It is not enough for you as a leader to have a goal or objective; you must be willing to pursue your goal or objective relentlessly with vigour and you can begin a crusade of change in your life and ministry by resolving to be a diligent person.

DISCIPLINE:

Discipline is another very important quality which an individual must possess as a leader. Every leader, irrespective of calling should and must strive to possess discipline as a dependable ally. Discipline as it is used in this material is not the same as receiving punishment for an offence committed. Discipline in this context, refers to the act of self-denial, or self-control. It is a calculated measure adopted by an aspiring individual who strongly desire to achieve success in life. Discipline is a self-imposed standard and restriction motivated by a desire that is greater than the alternatives.

It is self-policing. For an individual who desires to lead people in whatever capacity must first be willing, and be able to lead himself (self- control) before he can successfully lead other people. Any leader that lacks control over his emotions and self in general may curse and quarrel with his followers/team; or even engage them in physical combat. Such leader could equally fall prey to seductive appeals from the opposite sex or embezzle the ministry, church/fellowship, or organization fund and may have real problem balancing his accounts due to impulsive (unbudgeted) expenses.

A leader must lead by showing good example to his followers. The leader's public life must not be different from his private life. I hear some people said "its government thing, Na mine Papa work?"

"A leader who is morally upright in the public, but fails to measure up to this same high standard in his private life, is guilty of double dealings: and this leader has a case to answer!"

Are you a leader and you are good at office/work place but when it comes to home thing, it becomes equivalent to Fuji house of commotion. You got a case to answer!

Discipline is an ancient art that is still very relevant and desirable in our modern world. Discipline as an art should be cultivated, developed and practiced. For instance, in the sporting world, athletes who desire to be champions are quite aware that winning the gold medal starts from the training practice. These athletes subject themselves to rigorous and strenuous discipline in order to put their physique in perfect shape. A leader in the household of faith must not only preach discipline to his member/followers, but he must also walk the talk i.e. lead by example by putting his preaching into practice. That is, the leader must also be a much disciplined person in order to be able to command the respect of his members/followers.

"...No man that wars entangles himself
with the affairs of this life..."
(2 Tim. 2:4.)

It takes discipline for a leader to discover his weakness and set out to correct or do something about them. A leader, who is not always punctual, must also expect the same result of poor time management from his followers. It is only natural because what you sow is what you are going to reap when it comes to harvest season! A person who is always procrastinating, putting off till another time what he has to do now, cannot be a good result oriented leader. This kind of person is lazy and cannot be trusted by his followers, because of his poor attitude to time. Time is very precious. Nobody has all the whole time in the world. Discipline ensures a judicious use of time for the purpose of accomplishing a set goal or objective. In fact, leader and time management shall be discussed in our subsequent chapter.

<u>THE PRICE OF DISCIPLINE:</u> Discipline would cost you something: it has a price which everyone who desires to be a leader must be willing to pay. Discipline would cost you self denial to be properly focused in pursuant of one's set objectives and goals, the individual who desires to be a leader must discipline himself by refusing to take part in certain pleasures and past time. Paul's advice is very instructive in these regards:

"...Remember that in a race everyone run's, but only one person gets the prize. You also must run in such a way that you will win. All athletes practice strict self control they do it to win a prize that will fade away but we do it for an eternal prize. So I run straight to the goal with purpose..."
(I Cor. 9:24-27 NLT).

A leader has so many things competing for his attention at the same time. If the leader fails to prioritize, he would be tempted to chase so many things at the same time. And, at the end, his maximum output in terms of results achieved, would absolutely be nothing when compared to the amount of valuable time and energy wasted, in this case, "strategy plus energy equal to tragedy". What a pity! This is where the leader has to exert much discipline on himself by cutting off unnecessary frivolities, thereby focusing his attention on things or matters that are very urgent and utmost importance. A man with a clear vision and dedicated commitment live a focused life which requires self discipline. This helps to determine the following:

- How he choose his priorities.
- How he invests his time.
- How he invests his money.
- The movies he watches.
- The books he reads and the things he listens to.
- The friends he keeps.

Praying and fasting, for example, is one area the leader has to allow himself to be discipline. It is quite unfortunate to see leaders frown and cry when you mention to them about fasting and praying. This is when they will remember their long forgotten ulcer, that is when they want to be busier, and want to travel for an important programme they say. Spiritual exercise, like praying, fasting, or reading and meditating on the word of God is highly demanding; and sometimes, very strenuous and physically exerting. The leader has no choice but to observe these spiritual exercises, if he must succeed as a leader in the household of faith (Church/fellowship). The early apostle of our Lord Jesus Christ recognized this important truth when they decided to focus their time and energy on their top most priority:

"...But we will give ourselves continually to prayer and to the ministry of the word..." (Acts 6:4)

Discipline is a necessary rod that everyone of us must apply constantly on ourselves, if we are truly desirous in becoming leaders of men and resources. Success in any leadership capacity or position is a combination of many important factors, such as discipline and hard work. A successful leader is a disciplined leader. As a leader, or an aspiring candidate for leadership position in life, you have an important part to contribute to your success; you must cultivate a disciplined life, and regulate your thoughts and activities based on the result you desire to achieve. You must begin now to identify your areas of weakness, and work on them by painstakingly applying the rod of discipline on yourself.

<u>SPIRITUAL DISCIPLINE</u>: Discipline is the measure taken to ensure conformity to the accepted standard. The Bible distinguished between chastening (discipline) and punishing

> ***"...Behold, happy is the man whom God correcteth..."***
> (Job 5:17)

Discipline is used only for God's people. It is a sure evidence of love and it has a goal "the development of a character in the person corrected". As a leader or one aspiring to be a leader someday, do you take pleasure when chastised? The focus of discipline is on training, instructing, correcting and improving. It is often accomplished through pain, sorrow and at times loss. On the other hand, punishment has flogging or death sentence as its penalty. On divine level, God punishes any and all sins with death, both physical and spiritual (eternal) death.

In the above scripture were we read, God is bold to declare openly "Behold, happy is the man whom God corrects" the question here is; Do we allow God to correct us as a leader or aspiring leader? We were ones told during our intake course at Enugu, Assemblies of God Secretariat, at the Royal Rangers Nigeria (RRN) officers National Drill Course, that we should see punishment (Drill) as part of worship to God for instance; if you were asked to fall like a dead man, you must do it not considering where you are and the ground; you will fall look but looking unto God, you feel nothing little wonder David said;

"...your rod and staff bring comfort to me..." (Psalms. 23: 4)

Many times, God corrected us through His word, men of God and leaders so that our lives could be in conformity to the accepted standard of God but we absconded, opted out and despised the correction. As a leader or aspiring leader, allow God to correct you so that you could be useful to your world, the people you are leading. The goal of God's discipline is for us to be conformed to the image of His Son Jesus Christ (Roman 8:29)

To be happy as a leader, believer or intending leader, never you despise the chastening of the Almighty. Spiritual discipline paves way for spiritual growth and improvement. If you must go further, as a leader, you must embrace chastening from men that are ahead of you. As a great and true leader, accept corrections from anyone in good faith, for it propels God's blessings in your leadership. And as you yield yourself to be corrected (discipline) the sky will not be your limit but Heaven.

HUMILITY

The Lord Jesus Christ spoke a whole lot in parable to people while he was on earth. One of such parable is the story of two men, a Pharisee (I call these group; "far to see-Jesus"), but that is by the way; a Pharisee, and a tax collector, who went to pray in the temple. The Pharisee, while praying was very busy boasting of all his achievements before God; how he pays his tithes and fast twice in a week. Meanwhile, the tax collector was also busy praying, but was so concerned for his soul, pleading that God would have mercy on him. The Lord Jesus Christ concluded his parable by saying that the tax collector went out of the presence of God to his home justified than the Pharisee.

> *"...for everyone that exalts himself shall be abased,*
> *and he that humbles himself shall be exalted..."*

Humility is a virtue to be pursued by everyone who aspires to be a leader; or who is already functioning in any leadership capacity. Humility is the opposite of pride and arrogance. An ancient ruler in Israel, King Herod died and was eaten-up by worms because he refused to humble himself before God, hence God humbled him to death. A leader who wants to continue to enjoy the support and patronage of his followers must learn to walk in humility. *Leadership Is A Call To Service*. The leader must serve his followers or the people that he is leading in humbleness of heart. A true leader is a servant leader. The Lord Jesus Christ is a perfect example of a leader who brought love, joy, and peace to His followers' through His service to humanity. The Lord Jesus Christ though a leader, came not to be served, but to serve.

> *"...Let this mind be in you, which was also in*
> *Christ Jesus; who, being in the form of God thought*
> *it not a thing to be grasped to be equal with God; But*
> *made himself of no reputation, and..."* (Phil. 2:5-8).

If Jesus Christ, who is our Lord and Master has to humble Himself in order to accomplish His purpose on earth. It is only logical that everyone who is called by His name should follow in His steps.

<u>THE CALL TO HUMILITY</u>: Humility is an integral aspect of good leadership. A leader or an individual aspiring for leadership position must be willing to accept, and also pay close attention to the demand of humility.

- The leader must recognize his limitations as an individual by submitting himself, and, walking before God in humbleness of heart.

"...He has showed you, O man, What is good; and what does the Lord require of you, but to do justly, and to love mercy, and to walk humbly with your God?" (Micah 6: 8)

- The leader, or the aspiring individual for leadership must be willing to work in humility before other people; especially the people under the authority of the leader.

"...Be completely humble and gentle; be patient bearing with one another in love..." (Eph. 4:2 NIV)

Humility will demand on the leader to always look beyond his personal worth as individual by recognising the importance and contributions of other people, especially those under his authority. It takes humility to recognize the fact that one can be wrong by accepting corrections from other people.

"...Do nothing out of selfish ambition or vain conceit, but in humility consider others better than yourselves..."
(Phil. 2:3)

Pretending to be humble, in order to have our way will only expose our insincerity to public ridicule. The leader must genuinely reflect true humility. Is not by saying it, in fact, your humility is in doubt, the moment you recognize or measure how humble you are to the people. Some even use this word as in "bros, or chairman, I dey loyal o!" The moment you use your mouth to confess your loyalty, becomes the moment you started showing your lack of loyalty. That is to saying that you are indirectly not loyal to them in the first place but only covering up with a verbal pretence.

> *"...therefore, as God's Chosen People, Holy and Dearly Loved, Clothe yourselves with Compassion, Kindness, Humility, Gentleness and Patience..."* (Col. 3:12 NIV)

<u>THE DIVIDENDS OF HUMILITY</u>: God has not called us to walk in humility in vain. The leader, who obeys God by walking in humility and faithfully fulfilling his mandate through purposeful and dedicated service in God's Kingdom, will definitely reap the rewards and blessings of humility.

■ <u>The backing and assurance of the grace of God</u>:

Without the Grace of God, The Leader becomes Empty; Devoid of Divine Enablement, Empowerment and Direction. *"He mocks proud mocker but gives grace to the humble"* (Prov. 3:34 NIV).

■ <u>The leader who walks in humility is assured of God's protection and security</u>:

Throughout my period of leadership till date, God has been divinely protecting and securing me. My leadership series were divine because in almost all of the occasion, I always stand to be the smallest. My contenders will always say; "this small boy will rule, lead or head us? They even went as far to threaten me but in all, I overcame because I was humble even in my exalted position as a small boy (Kekere). That, you can also enjoy if you render your service to all in humility. In times of severe testing and trials, God fights for the humble in heart.

"You save the humble but bring down
whose eye are haughty".

■ **<u>The leader who obeys God by walking in humility is a candidate of divine elevation and honour</u>:**

"The fear of the Lord is the instruction of wisdom, and before honour is humility" (Proverbs 15:33)

■ **<u>The person or leader who walks in humility is greatly rewarded by the Almighty God</u>:**

"By humility and the fear of the Lord are riches, and honour, and life". (Proverbs 22:4)

■ **<u>The humble at heart or the leader who walks in humility is assured of the wisdom, which comes from God</u>:**

Wisdom separates an individual from the crowed; wisdom ensures distinction and promotion for a leader who walks in humility.

"...When pride comes, then disgrace, but with
humility comes wisdom..." (Proverb 11:12 NIV)

■ **<u>The leader, who is humble at heart, has a teachable Spirit</u>:**

It is very easy for such an individual to receive instruction and direction from God.

> *"...He guides the humble in what is right and*
> *teaches them His way..."* (Proverb 25:9 NIV)

Humility has it dividends. To qualify for the benefits of humility, we have to learn it. Do you want to be a leader; or are you already functioning, in a leadership capacity? Do you wish to be more effective and fruitful as a leader? The choice is really yours! You can begin to put into practice (because practice they say, make improvement) what you have learnt in this book/chapter. Humility is a price you have to pay if you must succeed as a leader with a prize.

<u>INTEGRITY:</u>

The leader who truly desires to lead and soar high in whatever capacity, calling or assignment he/she finds himself or herself, must be ready and willing to cultivate, develop, possess, and put into practice this essential leadership quality called Integrity. "integrity" as one of the qualities a leader or aspiring leader must develop and possess is to being honest; having a high standard of moral value and principle;

> *"...the man of integrity walks securely, but*
> *he who..."* (Proverb 10:9 NIV)

The leader who is a man of integrity would not have cause or reason to be afraid of the people that he is leading.

A leader of integrity would inspire trust and confidence among the people he is leading. Integrity binds the heart of the leader with the hearts of his followers. The people that are following the leader are easily convinced of the transparent honesty and sincerity of their leaders. And, because of this visible characteristic of the leader, the people are ever willing to give their support and encouragement to the leader. The leader who is a man of integrity will be guided in the right direction;

> *"...the integrity of the upright guides them, but the unfaithful..."* (Proverb 11:3 NIV)

The leader who is not straight forward and honest cannot be totally trusted by his followers. This kind of leader will end up having problems and eventually discredited. God is always looking for a man of integrity; such a man attracts the blessing and protection of God. Moses was a man of integrity. He was greatly used of God in bringing the nation of Israel out of bondage in Egypt. Moses never did anything to further his own personal ambitions. Moses was interested in serving God by being a blessing to his people; the Israelite. God honoured Moses in the sight of all Israel because he walked before God in the integrity of his heart.

> *"...Righteousness guards the man of integrity, but wickedness over throws the sinner..." (Proverbs 13:6 NIV)*

> *"...I know, my God, that you test the heart and are pleased with integrity..."* (1Chrn. 29:17 NIV)

Integrity is the acid test of leadership. As a leader, if you lack integrity as an individual, your leadership lacks merit and, it is bound to fail. A leader that fails the test of integrity is already in trouble because, God, himself is not pleased with him/her. And you can imagine what will happen to a man that the Most High God is not pleased with.

> *"...When a man's ways please the Lord, he maketh even his enemies to be at peace with him..."* (Prov. 16:7)

A leader must lead by example: you must walk the talk; your followers should be able to vouch for your impeccable character. As a true leader, you can begin your journey into unending success by being honest, sincere and truthful, no matter what condition or situation you may find yourself. As a leader up in any leadership capacity, you must be up (keep leading) right (doing what is obtainable); upright; that is integrity.

We could go on and on to enumerate the qualities of leaders with character but let's summarize it to say that a leader have the following (a true and real leader to be precise):

- They have sound integrity
- They learn something new daily and keep to, mind what they have learnt before.
- They have vision; they always look forward to what life should be.
- They are discipline.
- They are diligent.
- They have humility.
- They have a can-do attitude; they believe anything is possible if it is right.
- They value people; they work in team. Team work is the beauty of Christ in action which convinces people to serve God together. As a team leader, you should know when there's a superior opinion over the former opinions.
- They initiate change; they don't wait for things to happen. They make things happen.
- They empower others; they contribute positively to the lives of others.
- They are accountable; they have the sense of accountability and responsibility to the dream, vision, purpose, and people attached to its assignment. A

True leader readily embraces submission to authority and is conscious of the stewardship of the trust given to him by those he is leading.

> ***"...It is required in stewardship that a
> man be found faithful..."***
> (1 Cor. 4:2).

As a leader, imbibe these qualities today and you are on your trip to becoming a respectable leader.

CHAPTER FIVE

L eadership is a calling. It is an instrument to power and authority ordained by God for effective administration and coordination of human affairs on earth. The word of God (Bible) affirms that the Almighty God rules in the affairs of men, and He (God) also appoints anyone He desires to rule over men. (Daniel 5:21)

The importance of leadership cannot be over-emphasized. It is very crucial in any human endeavour for progress and development. And that is why in this chapter (Five), the focus would be on the functional aspects of leadership. Having known what leadership is all about, who a leader is, the making of a leader and the qualities with character of a leader. Let us take a trip to practical application of leadership (functional leader) otherwise known as showing working in leadership.

DECISION-MAKING:

Decision-making is the responsibility of leadership. The weight of making decision squarely rests on the shoulders of a leader. The people or the followers of a leader look upon him for direction, or what to do. Without the leader, the led (followers) are like sheep without a shepherd. Decision-making is a process of incubating ideas and plans in the mind of a leader. It is a situation, whereby the leader thoroughly considers taking a step or action by deciding to stick out his neck on a particular matter(s). Life is a continuum (continuous process) of decision-making. We make decisions every day. What to eat, what to buy, what clothes, shoe to put on etc.

In the case of a leader, apart from making personal and natural decisions, for instance, who to marry, where to live, what course/profession to study etc; the leader also makes specific, sensitive and very critical decisions that has profound effects on the people that he is leading.

Moses was a leader in ancient Israel; during his leadership, his everyday life was replete with decision-making. The choice of sending twelve men to spy the land of Canaan was one of such decisions. Moses had to make decisions during his leadership in Israel.

> *"And the Lord spoke unto Moses, saying send men that they may search the land of Canaan, which I give unto the children of Israel of ..."* (Number 13:1-2)

The Lord God instructed Moses to send spies to the land of Canaan; it was his (Moses) responsibility to decide the men that will carry out God's instruction. Please get this right because a lot of persons will node their head that l should ride, just to say on to cover up his/her self-centred decision-making attitude which he/she exercises on his/

her team member just because   he/she is the team leader. For the fact that you're privileged to be the team leader does not make you an all knowing person, that your team members are not important in decision –making. That is an error arbiniteur. As a team leader, call your team members together to decide what to do in any issue. Even God called His team members.

"...And God said, let us make man..." (Genesis 1:26)

No good product is produced by one person. Decision-making is an integral function of a leader. The leader must be decisive and firm. David as a leader of a small band of men that followed him had an opportunity to kill Saul who was chasing him (David), not to promote or give him gift items but to kill him (David). Shockingly to know that against the wishes of his team (men), David decided to spare the life of Saul. As a leader, it was a very critical moment for David; His men (team members) saw the opportunity as God-given, yet, David stood his ground, by refusing to kill Saul, even though Saul was actually after David to kill him.

"...And he (David) said unto his men, The Lord forbids that I should do this thing unto my master..." (1 Samuel 24:6 -7)

<u>The Impacts of Decision–Making</u>: Decision-making results in either positive or negative actions. David as a leader in Israel decided to build a temple for God. This was a positive decision. God did not allow David to accomplish this mission; but, He (God) allowed Solomon, the son of David to build the temple. Saul as a king, leading the Israelite army was instructed by God through Prophet Samuel to destroy the Amalekites. Saul partially obeyed the commandment of God by deciding to spare Agag, the king of

the Amalekites. The effects of Saul's negative decision in sparing Agag, the king of the Amalekites brought about his subsequent dethronement as king of Israel (1Samuel 15:1-23) Goliath; the giant was a threat to the armies of Israel. At the camp of the Israeli, nobody wanted to fight the giant. Just then, David surfaced and decided to fight Goliath. There was another threat David had to deal with before confronting Goliath, Saul; the king almost discouraged David from going to fight the giant from the land of the Philistine.

> *"And Saul said to David, you are not able to go against this philistine to fight with him; for you are but a youth and he is a man of war from his youth."* (1Samuel 17:33)

David desperately had to convince Saul to allow him (David) fight Goliath. Saul's decision to allow David fight Goliath, the giant freed the Israeli from possible domination from the Philistines. (1Samuel 17:24 -51)

Decision-making is something a leader must never shy away from or be afraid to do. It is an integral part of leadership. What you need when taking or making any decision is God's wisdom and this can only be done through prayer and studying of the word of God. Know that the church, (you and me) is the only Army that march forward on their knees, so is the leader.

> *"Give me now wisdom and knowledge, that I may go out and come in before this people: for who can judge this thy people, that are so great?"* (2 Chronicles 1:10)

Decision-making is very important for a leader. This is an aspect that a leader must never shy away from.

The nature of your calling as a leader demands that you

must nurture it always by making positive and far reaching decisions that naturally nurture and affects the live of other people especially, those who are under your leadership.

<u>THE FATHER SECURITY</u>:

> *"...When he arose, he took the young child and his mother by night and departed..."* (Matthew 2:14)

To protect your destiny and that of your followers from suddenly disappearing, you need to take precaution. Matthew chapter 2 tells us of how God took precaution for the protection of Jesus Life and destiny. The wise men took precaution by not returning to Herod. Even Joseph took precaution. If you want to fulfil destiny, you need to keep yourself and that of your followers safe from attacks. Every child of destiny is always a target of the devil. He wanted to kill Jesus but he could not because of people like Joseph that took precaution. I am talking about proper parenting here in the aspect of fathering as a leader. Don't ignore this lesson because as a leader, you are like a father to your followers, in fact, some persons will call you papa, that is not because you birthed them, some of them are able to be your father by age, meanwhile, know that, you will one day be a parent. But if you are a father already, glory to God because you are also a leader.

A leader must be wise enough to protect his followers (children) from the jaws and claws of the enemy. A lot of leadership setting (families) are in shambles today because there are no responsible leaders (fathers). A lot of so-called leaders (fathers) don't know what their duties are. Leaders (fathers) are made to be sensors and protectors. If you as a leader (father) are too careless to expose your followers (family) to the attacks of the enemy, then you are prepared to lose them. As a leader (father), it is imperative for you to avoid carelessness, pride, ego selfishness, slumbering and worldliness in order to protect your followers (family) from the attacks of enemy. As a leader (father), you must be ready to take the followers (family) and lead them to the right place with good pasture. Joseph was not just a father, but a great and true father. "Every leader (father) must have a correct link with God if he will have a correct lead in his leadership (home). When the wise men came to greet baby Jesus, they saw Him and presented gift's to Him. These were nice times you know and Joseph really didn't have much to do here. But when the devil started raising his ugly head, Joseph had to, under God, rise up to protect the family–the young child and the mother from the plan of the enemy, so should a leader at all time, to avoid harm to the led. Let us not forget that Joseph at this point in time was self–employed but he didn't let his work extricate him from family. Some families (leadership) today are in disarray as a result of the fact that the couple (Leaders) are looking for money. The couple goes to work in the morning and return at 10:30pm and by the time they get home, the children have slept off. This can be dangerous to family health, so it is in leadership, a situation where the leader feels careless about his followers exposing them not enjoying the dividends due them as a legal member of your leadership. As a leader and a father, you must take and make critical decision that will sustain your people and their health. Take precaution in not allowing them get exposed to suffering that may serve as a pre-disposing factor to ill-health, then, by so doing, you are a great leader.

Problem–Solving

Problem–solving is an essential function of leadership. The continued relevance of a leader is hinged on his ability to solve the problems of his people (followers). A leader should show the way out through the dark tunnel. Life is replete with all kinds of problems. A problematic condition or situation for an individual may not exactly be the same for another individual. Problems differ with different categories of people.

This is why a leader must be careful and sensitive to the needs of his people or followers. The solution to a particular problem might not necessarily be the solution to another kind of problem. It is the leader's responsibility to bring comfort, hope, and encouragement to the people under his leadership.

It is also the responsibility of the leader not only to proffer solution to a particular problem (s) but, the leaders must ensure that the problem is actually taken care of by solving it. In fact, as a leader, you need to show working by solving or handling the matter squarely.

Know the Nature of the Problem: A leader must understand the nature of a problem, before he can successfully proffer solution to that problem. This is very important, because, without knowing exactly what the problem is, it is going to be very difficult to attempt solving the problem. A leader must be well-disposed, informed and very practical in his approach to issues or, problems confronting his people or followers. David found himself in a critical and very deplorable situation; his wives and children were taken captives; his place of abode, Ziklag was ransacked and burn with fire by foreign invaders; and to compound his troubles, David's men wanted to stone him, because of their own problems! As a leader, David having assessed the situation, had to brace-up by encouraging himself in God (1 Sam. 30:6). Sometimes, there are situations that come up, and the leader is left alone to confront the bull by the horn! The Bible records that:

"And David enquired at the Lord, saying, shall I pursue after this troop? Shall l overtake them? And he answered him, pursue: for thou shall surely overtake them..."
(1 Sam. 30:8).

David was very realistic in his assessment of the problematic condition he and his men found themselves. As a leader, he knew something had to be done in order to restore the confidence of his followers; their problem had to be solved! "And David recovers all that the Amalekites had carried..." (1 Sam. 30: 18-19).

Leaders are either appointed or elected to bring about positive changes in the lives of the people under their leadership. A leader who cannot effect practical changes, or bring about solutions to the problems of their organization, ministries, churches/ followership; cannot really be a leader. Leaders must not only lead, inspire, and motivate the people under their leadership; they must also be able to solve their problems.

Delegate Responsibilities and Functions:

Problem-Solving can also be effectively achieved through delegation of responsibilities and functions. This can be done in a situation, whereby, the leader decide to "share" his responsibilities by appointing or delegating some of his people or followers to function in a particular role or duty.

Moses could have weared himself out if he had not consented to the advice of Jethro, his father in-Law, to share his responsibilities to other capable individuals among his people, the Israeli.

> *"And Moses' father in-law said unto him, the thing that thou doest is not good. Thou will surely wear away..."* (Exodus 18:17-18, 21-22)

To facilitate solution to a problem and enhance the quality of pragmatic leadership, a leader must learn to assign duties and functions to his subordinates or assistants. By doing this, the leaders get the chance to solving the problems of a greater number of people. This is not the same with shying away from your responsibilities and functions but delegating some oversight functions so that other problems can be meet without delay to avert damage or worsening the situation besides, you cannot be everywhere at the same time. It even helps you to reproduce more competent leaders that will take over from you someday. But also don't use this delegating thing to cover your laziness in carrying out your official function because it is the order of the day now, where the leader sit aloof and command around his subordinates/assistant to do these and that; that is laziness arbiniteur.

A leader who cannot solve the problems of his organization, church, fellowship or ministry, cannot effectively lead or direct the people under his leadership. Leadership is responsibility. It is all about bringing positive impacts and changes in the lives of the people under the authority of a leader. Leadership is all about being pragmatic and result-oriented. A leader must inspire confidence, trust and motivate the people that he is leading. Leadership in general, is action; and being real to our followers.

PROBLEM-SOLVING... THE SHORTEST ROUTE TO LEADERSHIP

> ***"...So David triumphed over the philistine..."***
> (1Samuel 17:20-50 NLT)

The entire problem of any nation in the world revolves around leadership problem. And it is good to note that your ability to lead will determine your ultimate success in your endeavours. Success in life is not linked to formulas but to understanding of some underlying concepts. One of them is leadership. Leadership is the ability to inspire and influence a group of people to achieve a worthwhile goal. That is, leadership is competence-based and inspirational in nature. Leaders are made from problem-solving that is why problem–solving is the shortest route to leadership. It is the ability of an individual to solve a problem and gain mastery over the problem that determines whether the person will be a leader or not. However, it is important that the individual specialize in solving his or her problem first because becoming a leader starts from within you. This is what will inspire others to follow suits. It is somewhat unnatural to follow someone that is battling with problems. Never leave your own problem unsolved trying to help others.

Your ability to solve your own problem will automatically attract people who have the same problem that you have now solved. It gives you the credibility to lead. On your route to becoming leader, the scope of the problems you solve begins to change and you start developing a bigger capacity to solve bigger problems. Therefore, if you just sit down there, watching problems, leadership will surely pass you by. Also, on the path to leadership, understand that the key to progress in a national society is not the empowering of the upper class but the lower class.

"Every society will travel at the pace in which the least person in that society travels".

So if you have already started leading, never neglect the lower and least people in your team or around you. Influence them! They will definitely give your leadership a star colour. As a leader, look out for someone in your team that is considered the least or the average, Decide to be close to that brother/ sister and influence them till they get better. In so doing, you're helping them solve their problems that naturally would have been difficult for them to tackle all alone.

If you so much desire to be a leader in any leadership setting, don't pray anymore for God to send you a helper rather pray to God to send you someone to help (Solve his/ her problem) as this will catapult you to yours desired leadership position over-night.

CHAPTER SIX

<u>LEADERSHIP PITFALLS</u>

This book is a practical ground for leadership. It is mainly for practicing leaders and for individuals who are aspiring for leadership positions in the nearest future.

The main objective of this book is not farfetched. This book is to instruct and to show in practical terms what leadership entails. In this, I urge you all reading this piece of information about leadership to stay put and judiciously consume it. This book would not be fulfilling God's reason for which it was written without addressing or considering some reasons why leaders fall or identifying some leadership pitfall.

WHY LEADERS FAIL:

Leaders are not Super-Men that are infallible but by the grace of God and total submission to simple instructions from his word (Bible) and books like this, the leaders can tap wisdom to avoid those pitfalls. The following are some of the reasons why some leaders fail in the discharge of their duties and responsibilities.

<u>REASONS WHY LEADERS FAIL</u>

Lack of Vision: Some leaders do not have a clear-cut vision or plan of action. Since, they have distorted vision or programme, these leaders naturally fail because, they do not have a proper focus, or lack understanding of what they actually want to accomplish.

Mismanagement of Resources: Some leaders have a false notion of leadership. These leaders see themselves as larger-than–life. They believe nobody can question their authority and that it is their opportunity to be rich and better in life. And that is why they can afford to waste money and other resources by squandering it on less important personal projects or ventures. We have them all over us this day to the extent that it is now trying to be a normal phenomenon. Even Christians are trying to hijack this illicit act of the world. Child of God, Stop! Because if you do, you are already in the pit of the devil. Pit stricken.

Abuse of Power/Position: Some leaders are so power-drunk that they end up abusing the privilege of their position of leadership. The followers of these leaders become so resentful and may even work against their progress.

Disobedience to God's Laws/Commandment: The blatant disregard of God's injunctions and commandment is a major reason why some leaders fail. God honours any individual or person who honours him by obeying his word. Saul was removed as King in Israel, because of his disobedience to God's word.

Ineffective Work-Force: Some leaders surround themselves with the wrong people as their workers, advisers, and confidants. This, in turn has adverse effect on the leader's overall performance.

King Rehoboam failed, because he despised the advice of the elders.

Pride: Beside every proud leader or person there is a pit, if you look very well'. An old man told his son. There are some Success Transmitted Diseases-STD, that success can bring; of which one of them is Pride. No one becomes proud if they don't have an achievement to hold to in their lives. It is very easy to be humble when you have not really become something big or done something big and tangible in life. But can you mange success on the high position or high side of life? Success can bring some dangerous and critical relationship into your life. You becoming a leader will introduce some dangerous and critical relationships into your life because it will surely attract people. But please note that the greatest trick of the devil is to push a leader or man into a position of pride. When the devil does this, he no more fights the person because he has turned the person into an enemy of God. So every time a person is tempted to be proud, it is a sign that the devil wants to use the person to stop the work of God in the life of that person/man or leader. The devil cannot stop God but this is one of his tricks-pride.

Pride can stop God" pride will make the leader, or man to be an enemy of God.

> *"...God opposes the proud, but favours the humble"* (James 4:6 NLT)

God himself resist the proud, because of this, the leader will be proud to fail   because when the Almighty God resist you, who else will defend you. You're already in the pit.

"Pride goes before destruction..." (Proverbs 16-18 NLT)

As a leader, don't play game with pride because destruction is behind it. As a leader, do people find it easy to correct you? Take off that pride from you and you will never fall into any pit trust God!

SEXUAL IMMORALITY:

But do not let immorality or any impurity or greed even be named among you, as is proper among saints; and there must be no filthiness and silly talk, or coarse jesting, which are not fitting, but rather giving of thanks. (Eph. 5:3-4). Whatever God establishes, Satan will counterfeit. Where God establishes true love, counterfeit love characterizes Satan's children, those who are of the world. Just as true love characterizes God's children, those who are citizens of heaven.

In contrast to Godly, unselfish, forgiving love, the world's is lustful and self-indulgent. It loves because the object of love is attractive, enjoyable, pleasant, satisfying, and appreciative, loves in return, produce desired feelings, or is likely to repay in some way. It is always based on the other person's fulfilling one's own needs and desires and meeting one's own expectations. Worldly love is reciprocal, giving little in much. Speaking of that kind of love, Jesus said,

"...for if you love those who love you, what reward have you? Do not even the tax-gatherers do the same? (Matt. 5: 46)

The world claims to want love, and love is advocated and praised from every corner. Romantic love especially is touted. Songs, novels, movies, and television serials continually exploit emotional, lustful desires as if it were genuine love. Questing for fantasizing about the "Perfect Love" is portrayed as the ultimate human experience.

It should not be surprising that the misguided quest for

that kind of love is selfish and destructive, a deceptive counterfeit of God's love. It is always conditional and is always self-centred. It is not concerned about commitment but only satisfaction; it is not concerned about giving but only getting. It has no basis for performance because its purpose is to use and to exploit rather than to serve and help. It lasts until the one loved no longer satisfies or until he or she disappears for someone else.

Porneia (Immorality) refers to all sexual sin and all sexual sin is against God and against godly love. It is the antonym of enkrateia, which refers t self-control, especially in the area of sex. When Paul spoke before Felix and his wife Drusilla "discussing righteousness, self-control, and the judgment to come, Felix became frightened and said, 'Go away for the present, and when I find time, I will summon you' " (Acts 24:24-25). Felix had stolen Drusilla from her former husband and was therefore living with her in an adulterous relationship. The sexual self-control of which Paul spoke pertained to lustful passion, as Felix understood. The message to the governor was that he was living contrary to God's righteousness by refusing to discipline his sexual desire, and for that he was subject to God's judgment.

As a leader or one who intend to be a leader; know it well that loss of sexual self-control leads to its opposite, which is immorality and impurity which is one of the most common pitfall of most renowned leaders.

Akatharsia (impurity) is a more general term than porneia, referring to anything that is unclean and filthy. Jesus used the word to describe the rottenness of decaying bodies in a tomb (Matt. 23:27). The other ten times the word is used in the New Testament is associated with sexual sin. It refers to immoral thoughts, passions, ideas, fantasies, and every other form of sexual corruption.

Contemporary sex madness has even found its way into some leadership setting, churches/ fellowships, and ministries as the case maybe because of the increased rate of morally imbalanced or immorality stricken leaders in our society today. The influence of the lustful world has been so pervasive and the church/ fellowships and ministries so weak and undiscerning that many Christians have become convinced that all sorts of sexual excesses and impurities are covered by grace or can be rendered morally safe if engaged in with the right attitude- especially if some scripture verse can be twisted to give seeming support. But sexual immorality and impurity cannot be sanctified or modified into anything better than what they are which is wickedness-a crime against the holy God and the loving Saviour. In (1Corinthians 5:1-5 and 6:13-20), Paul shows that there is no place for that in the Christian life.

As mentioned under the discussion of Ephesians 4:19, greed is inseparable from impurity. Every form of sexual immorality is an expression of self-will, self-gratification, and self-centredness of greed. It is by nature contrary to love, which is self-giving. As a leader, stay away from it.

Immorality and impurity are but forms of greed in the realm of sexual sin. They are manifestation of sexual covetousness and express counterfeit love (which is really hate, since love seeks the purity of others and is unselfish) masquerading as something beautiful, good, and rewarding. Because those sins seems so attractive and promising, spouses are forsaken, children are neglected, homes are destroyed, friends are disregarded, ministries, churches and fellowships are blurred of God's presence and glory, as no effort is spared to fulfil the desire to have the one who is lusted after- all of that in the name of love triggered by that so-called morally imbalanced leader. This pitfall is not only to the leader but also to the led/ followers are also in the mess of heartbreak. As a leader or intending leader, instead of being involved in sexual immorality and or filthy speaking, the leader's mouth should be involved in the giving of thanks. Thanksgiving is an expression of unselfishness. The selfish and unloving person does not give thanks because he thinks he deserves whatever good thing he receives. The unselfish and loving leader on the other hand, focuses his life and his concern on the needs of others/ his followers. He is always thankful because his spirit is one of loving and of giving. Instead of using others, he serves them. Instead of trying to turn the innocent into the immoral, he seeks to change the immoral into what is righteous and holy. He is thankful because the holy life is the satisfying life, and people (followers) see love for God in the thankful leader/person. May God increase you in grace as a leader to lead by example.

LOVE FOR MONEY:

As Nigerian Christians, living in a state where even the government runs ads enticing us to gamble, we need to consider carefully the Apostle Paul's words, ***"But those who want to get rich fall into temptation and a snare and many foolish and harmful desires which plunge men into ruin and destruction, for the love of money is a root of all sort of evil, and some by longing for it have wandered away from the faith, and pierced themselves with many a pang"*** (1Tim. 6:9-10).

Commentators are quick to point out that Paul is often

misquoted as, "Money is the root of all evil." It is not money, but the love of it that is a root of evil. They say, our money isn't the problem but our attitude towards it. We all hear this and exclaim, "Wow! I guess I'm okay, then, because I have the right attitude toward money." But not so fast! As a leader or soon to be leader, while money may be neutral, we need to realize that it is dangerous. "The reason money is dangerous is the same reason loaded guns are dangerous: they both can be used only by one kind of people (fallen sinners): both money and loaded guns can be quite useful in certain situations if you're careful. There's nothing I would rather have than a loaded gun if an angry beer was chasing me in the forest. But even so, I would better treat it with respect and know how to use it or could harm me or my loved ones as much as the beer could. Money deserves the same caution as a loaded gun: if you're not careful, it can destroy you and your followers (family)! Paul is telling us as a leader that...

"The desire for money will deceive and ultimately destroy you"

Paul outlines a three step process:

1. **The *desire* for money;**

2. **The *deception* of money;**

3. **The *destruction* caused by money.**

The desire draws you in; the deception gets you comfortable and oblivious to the danger; the destruction polishes you off. This pattern is followed in verse 9 and repeated in verse 10 of 1 Timothy for emphasis (D^3):

1. The *desire*: "want to get rich" (verse 9), "Love of money" (verse 10);
2. The *deception*: "snare" (verse 9), "wandered

away" (verse 10);

3. The *destruction*: "ruin and destruction" (verse 9), "away from the faith", "pierced themselves with many a pang" (verse 10).

1. **THE DESIRE**: *The decision to pursue riches is a root of sin.*

In Greek, "root," is placed first in the sentence for emphasis. The love of money is not the only root of evil, but it is a powerful one. Philips paraphrases it: "for loving money leads to all kinds of evil".

DEFINITION: What does Paul mean by "the love of money"? Does he mean that it's wrong to enjoy material things? Are we sinning if we purchase and actually enjoy anything above the bare necessities of life? If that were so, Paul would not state in verse 17 of 1Timothy chapter 6 that God "richly supplies us with all things to enjoy". Here's a definition I came up with as I pondered Paul's words: the love of money is a decision or desire to pursue wealth for personal consumption and luxury. The love of money can be either a deliberate decision ("want to", verse 9) or a desire (=lust, verse 9) that hasn't been carefully thought through. In either case, the person has a goal in life to make a lot of money so that he can enjoy life in style. The goal may stem from a lack of contentment, which in turn may be due to not having the purpose of godliness or the perspective of eternity (as we can read through from verse 6-8). It may stem from *"the lust of the flesh, the lust of the eyes, and the boastful pride of life"* (1John 2:16), which tempt us all. But the love of money is an aim, a goal, a focus.

As with all lusts, there's an emotional element to it. It's not completely rational. It tugs at you from inside. The person "Longs for" money (verse 10). The Greek word means to stretch oneself out, to reach after, and to inspire to. It is used positively of a man aspiring to the office of elder (1 Tim. 3:1). It points to an inner desire. The word Paul used for "Love for money" (Philarguria= Love of Silver) points to the love of emotion and friendship (Phileo). So we're talking about a goal that sometimes is a deliberate choice, and sometimes just a strong inner longing to be rich. It stands in opposition to the contented Christian whose aim is godliness because his focus is on eternity, not on this fleeting world.

Often, this desire for wealth stems from pride, which the Christian world now erroneously labels "Low self-esteem" the person is seeking the affirmation and status that wealth brings. He needs to prove to himself and others that he really is somebody, and one way to do that is to make a lot of money, live in luxury, and impress people. Biblically, the person doesn't need "proper self-esteem", but to judge his pride and self-focus, and to find contentment in God. Because all of us are prone to pride, we all need to be on guard against the love of money. They go hand in hand.

<u>THE PRINCIPLE</u>: *The root determines the fruit.*

The love of money is a root sin. That is to say; it lies beneath the surface and nourishes any number of other sins. The root in this case bears several kinds of fruit. But whatever the variation, the fruit is sin because the root is sin. The root determines the fruit. Hear this! You are free to choose the root, but not the fruit. You are free to plant any kind of seed you want in your yard this spring (your spring here could be your period of reign as a leader). But once they take root, you're not free to pick a different kind of fruit. If you plant an apple tree, you may not later pick peaches. We've got some weeds in our yard that send down tap roots that could support a tree. Once those weeds take root, they spread and will take over your entire yard if you let them. If evolution and survival of the fittest were true, these weeds would have taken over the world before animal life ever came into existence! If you let the love of money take root, it's like those weeds, it will dominate you and in the end, you will reap ruin and destruction.

Think, ponder or mutter through the Ten Commandments (Exodus 20:3-17). The love of money (or covetousness, the tenth commandment) can be the root cause of breaking the other nine.

Commandment 1: you shall have no other gods before me. Jesus said; "you cannot serve God and mammon" either money is your god, or God is your God.

Commandment 2: "you shall not make for yourself an idol..." *Col. 3:5*, "greed, which amounts to idolatry".

Commandment 3: "you shall not take the name of the Lord your God in vain". How many people have cursed when they have a lot of money?

Commandment 4: "keep the Sabbath day holy. Many are too busy pursuing riches to set aside one day each week for the Lord.

Commandment 5: "Honour your father and mother." It is commonly ignored for the love of money!

Commandment 6: "you shall not murder". How often murder is because of money!

Commandment 7: "you shall not commit adultery." How often woman goes after another woman's husband because she wants his money!

Commandment 8: "you shall not steal". Robbery, theft, and fraud wouldn't exist if people do no love money.

Commandment 9: "you shall not bear false witness". How many lie in order to make money!

So the **Tenth Commandment**; "you shall not covet," is indeed, a root sin that can lead to many other sins. The first step toward destruction is when we don't root out of our hearts the weed called "the love of money" as a leader. Covetousness equals idolatry (Col. 3:5).

2. *THE DECEPTION: The delusion of riches follows the desires.*

The desire draws you in. If you don't confront your love of money and yank it by the roots every time you see it spring up in another corner of your life as a leader, it will delude you until it takes over and destroys you.

Note verse 9: "Fall into temptation and a snare". "Fall into" is used of an animal falling into a pit. A snare points to something hidden and unexpected. In verse 10, the word "Wandered away" comes from a root word meaning to go astray, often with the thought of deception. So the picture is that of an unsuspecting animal stepping on some branches only to discover, too late, that they cover a deep pit. The animal falls in and is trapped. The reason the pursuit of riches deceives is that money does not last and it never brings true happiness. You can be as wealthy as Mr. Aliko Dangote was, but it won't extend your life if you get terminal cancer.

> *"Money will buy a bed but not sleep; books but not brains; food but not appetite; finery but not beauty; a house but not a home; medicine but not health; luxuries but not culture; amusements but not happiness; religion but not salvation; a passport to everywhere but not to heaven".*

I came to discovered, to my amusement, that undertakers are sometimes called on to provide suitable clothing for the diseased to be buried in. They make special suits for such occasions that look just like ordinary suits, except that they have no pockets. Their customers don't have any need for pockets. They don't bring anything into this world, and they're not taking anything with them. I was one day trekking through my usual road to school and saw an old time friend called Raymond. As we were strolling down the road, I tried to talk to him about the Lord. The conversation turned to wealth and the young man said, "I hope I can be like my uncle. He died a millionaire". I said, "what?" He said, "He died a millionaire". I said, "No, he didn't. The young man said, "what do you mean? I replied, Ray, "who has the million now? "He said, oh! I see what you mean". Money doesn't last. And it can't buy true happiness. Some of the most miserable people in this world are the entertainers who can buy anything they want, but they are lonely, alienated, unhappy people. Money can't bring true happiness because it can't reconcile us to God or to other people, because it doesn't deal with our sinful self-will that alienates us from God and others. Only Christ Jesus through His death on the cross can forgive our sins which is of course a proven fact that our sins are forgiven us (Matt. 9:3). Only Christ Jesus can deal the death-blow to our love of self as we enthrone Jesus as our rightful Lord. He said,

"If anyone wishes to come after me, let..." (Luke 9:23-25).

Because you are reconciled to God and to your follow man, you find that the benefit of this often painful process of death to self is life indeed. And because the love of money is really just a means toward the love of self, part of the daily process of death to self is crucifying the desire for riches which would have make as a leader to be so mean to people that seems blocking your desired expectation as to be rich. Thus first is the desire for riches. If we as leaders don't confront and crucify it every time it raises its ugly head on us, it leads to the deception of riches. Deception leads to destruction.

3. THE DESTRUCTION: *The deterioration and demise of the person is the final result.*

Note verse 9; "Plunge men into ruin and destruction". And verse 10; "Wandered away from the faith, and pierced themselves with many a pang". The word "Plunge" is used in Luke 5:7 of boats filled with fish beginning to sink. An overloaded but can stay afloat in calm seas, but any waves will swamp it and sink it to the bottom. A person pursuing riches can go along looking fine, but he isn't prepared for a crisis. He hasn't been living each day by trusting God and looking to Him, so when he is swamped by a catastrophe, he has nowhere to turn. He goes down.

Maybe you're thinking, "well, I'm not rich so this doesn't apply to me". But let me shock you that you're mistaken on two counts charge as a leader: In the first place, living in Nigeria means that even though you're poor by Nigerian standards, you're rich by some other countries. Second; Paul doesn't say, "those who are rich," but rather, "those who desire to get rich". Many times, those who lack money have more of a craving for it than those who have it. Paul's warning here is strong medicine, and although medicine sometimes, doesn't taste good, we need it to get well. As a leader or an individual who someday will assume leadership position, whatever your financial situation is, you are prone to the love of money because as I said earlier, it's tied in with the love of self to which we're all inclined. John Wesley remarked in life that he had known only four (4) men who had not declined in religion by becoming wealthy. At a later period in life he corrected the remark and made no exception. As a leader or an individual, do you love money? Remember, the desire for money will deceive you and leads to ultimate ruin. Flee from these things, oh you leader, man or woman of God.

<u>ANGER:</u>

Often times, angry people usually justify their anger, saying its someone else's fault they are angry. And I keep asking myself a thousand times this question, "to who is the anger credited? Who receives the pain? Hurt or heartbreak at last?" the same angered person of course! Yet the Bible repeatedly warns us against giving in to anger when we are upset by other people's words or actions. As leaders, sometimes, we need to talk about problems or deal with dangerous situations. Even at this period or time of our life, we must exercise self-control. Yet most of the time, our anger is not righteous neither will it make us righteous. As James wrote,

> ***"Man's anger does not bring about the righteous life that God desires"*** (James 1:20).

When we give in to anger, we often focus on our own welfare, comfort or happiness. Instead, we should be primarily concerned about other people's welfare and being a true leader and good witness to God. As you can see in the following scriptures; God does not want us to simply react emotionally to other's actions, hence it will land us to pitfall as leader. Instead, we should respond with wisdom and a gentle spirit.

As a leader or intending leader, never show your anger at once during your leadership setting, though there may be some situation that will give you thousands of reasons to do so but as a true and good leader, display your prudent charisma in overlooking that insult.

> ***"A fool shows his annoyance at once, but a prudent***

man (leader) overlooks an insult". (Prov. 12:16)

As a leader, *"your escape route to pitfall is your escape means to anger"* and as you rid yourself of it, the sky will be your starting point.

SOME LEADERS THAT FAILED:

Samson and Saul are two of a kind. They were both leaders in Israel. Samson was a Warrior-Judge who terrorized the Philistines, the enemies of Israel. Samson, as a leader led a reckless and fearless life. As a Nazareth, Samson never regarded his vows. Samson was eventually captured and his eyes plucked out by his enemies while he was relaxing on the laps of a woman, called Delilah! What a shame for a war Lord to be stripped of his eyes on a woman's laps.

Saul was also a warrior, chosen to be King over the nation of Israel. Throughout his tenure as King, he battled with the philistines, the enemies of Israel. Saul also disobeyed God's commandment, and he paid dearly with his life! Saul died in a battle, and another man occupied his position as King.

King Solomon's thousand burnt offerings and a thousand women (700 wives and 300 concubines). He failed due to negative influence from strange women during his old age. Also, King David's adultery, murder and pride (for numbering Israelites without God's approval). Every leader who wants to achieve success in whatever leadership position or capacity must never follow the lifestyle of Samson and Saul. Sin is a dangerous pitfall every leaders who desires to succeed must avoid at all cost! Don't spoil your reputation, destiny, glory for just that one scene action. Don't mortgage your future for just that one scene pleasure that will not last.

> *"Lo, this is the man that made not God his strength;*
> *but trusted in the abundance of his riches, and*
> *strengthened himself in his weakness"* (Psalm 52:7)

Sin is a dangerous pitfall every leader must avoid at all cost. If, you fail to deal with sin, the repercussions of sin will certainly catch up with you. Sin is an enemy; it is never a friend! We must all learn from the mistakes of leaders who failed when it mattered most to God. God wants you to succeed, and that, is why He has raised you up as a leaders. You must not fail God in your own generation. If you fail to deal with sin, sin will not fail to deal with you. Pitfall!!! Beware!!!

CHAPTER SEVEN

YOUR ROLE IN YOUR TEAM

A team is a group comprising people with complementary skills who are working for common purpose to which they are collectively accountable"- according to John Child. A team is a group of people with a commitment to one another, to the high level of accomplishment of a goal and a common vision. The human body is a well constructed entity. God did a perfect work in constructing it. The body is one, but with many parts, in which some are internal and some are external. There are internal organs in the body that we don't see, yet we cannot do without. The heart is one of them; life stops when it stops.

The size of the heart proves that it is not the size of a thing that totally determines its effectiveness or functionality because the size of heart of all of us is the size of our fists. Another very effective organ in the body is the eye. It is the light of the body. There are many other organs in the body that make the body functions effectively. Most times, the best way to know how important these organs are is when a body is afflicted with sickness. It is the body organs that determine the effective functionally of the body. Sound health means all the organs of the body are functioning well. So also is the human team that you are in. That team is a body while your presence in that team makes you one of the organs. As a team member, you must understand your role and importance to your team. As no organ or part of the body is superior to another organ or part of the body, so also, no team member is superior to another team member; all team members are organs in the team body. If you as one of the organs in the team body are not doing your work, what is really expected of you, you ultimately make the team sick. Also, if it is another team member that is not working or working well, the team becomes sick.

In order to understand your role in your team, first note that your role in that team is not in any way inferior, especially if you are not the head of the team (team leader). Note that the head of the body is also a part of the body, any head you see alone without the body is dead. So also the head of your team is an organ in the team body. Your major role in your team is to build up the vision of your team. Your major contribution to the team should be to be committed to making the vision of the team a reality. That is one major thing that you will be remembered for as team member. So be wise. Pray for the vision; support the visionary, sacrifice for the vision, contribute to the vision, encourage the vision and stir up the team members in the path of the vision. That was exactly what Joshua did, with Caleb as his assistant, under the leadership of Moses.

When all Israel had gotten discouraged and Moses still had the vision to take the Israelite to the Promised Land. That was why when Moses was about to die, there was nobody God could choose to replace Moses. God had to choose

Joshua.

Numbers 13:14 has the details of what happened as it teaches us as a team member to learn your own roles, not only the rules in your team.

Roles here means, those contributions, support, sacrifice and services you render to your team as a whole to fulfil God's plan (purpose and vision of the team) whereas rules here implies doing those laid down functions, duties all alone not minding the business of the other team members.

For instance, The Vice President do nothing but wait until the president is not around, while in the team, are a whole lot of functions to assist, but simply because the rules states that the Vice President is to function in the absence of the President, I don't think these kind of Jamboree should be seen in teamwork because the language of teamwork is "We", "Our", "Us" rather than "I", "Mine", "Me". As a team member, don't say because you're not a prayer leader hence cannot mobilize people for it when the need arise, as a team member don't say because you're not the sister's coordinator hence cannot coordinate the sister's when the need arise etc or even as a sister' coordinator, prayer coordinator or whatever. If someone else in your team carryout duties, to ensure the work is not lagging behind, you start to read and grumble in heart that someone has or is crossing boundary or the person must have taken permission to carry out an emergency function to keep the work of God going. This issue is mostly seen among sister's team member. I'm not saying that taking/obtaining permission to carry out some function when you have a leading from above (God), is wrong, but in emergency situation were something urgent must be some need not to be seen as abuse of office, violation of office, neglect of office or position or crossing of boundary among team members for the purpose of team work. As a leader or a team member in any leadership cadre, decide today never to function below what is expected of you in the team you are in.

THE LEADER AND FRIENDS:

As iron sharpens iron, so a friend sharpens a friend" (Prov. 27:17, NLT). As a leader in any leadership settings, you need to be careful with the kind of friends you keep, don't mortgage your purpose in life with your choices of friends. Your friends determine your end. They will either make or mar you, they will either "Promote or Pro-mute (demote) you".

A story was once told about a teacher of an elementary class who entered his class to teach his pupils English Language. He asked the pupils to rise up. They did. Then he asked the pupils to come out and stay in front of the class, one of the boys came out. The teacher handed over the white board marker to the boy and asked him to write the word "FRIEND" on the white board. The boy wrote it excellently and won the applause of the whole class.

Furthermore, the teacher, wanting to explain something to the class, called on another pupil, but this time around, a girl came out. The teacher told her to clean off the first three letters of the word written by the other boy, the whole class stood aghast, Thinking "what is Mr. Smart trying to bring out?" Without minding what the pupils were thinking, the girl went ahead and wiped off the first three letters. Mr. Smart turned to the pupils and asked them to spell and pronounce what is left after the first three letters have been wiped off. The whole class chorused END. The pupils looked at one another in silence and awe. Then he broke their silence, "choose your FRIEND wisely because your friend can determine your END in life'. As a leader or even as a follower or a team member, choose your friends wisely because they (friends) can determine your end, they can Make or Mar you. They can Promote you or Promute (Demote) you in life.

Amnon, being King David's first born, was supposed to be the king after David. But his friend Janadab gave him ''Ota-Pian-pian (wrong advice) as advice that led to his premature and untimely death (1 Sam. 13)

Today, look at your friends, I mean, your friendship as a person / individual, look out for the values of your friend in your life. What do they like in you that attracted them to yourself? Or what do you see in them that got you attracted to them? What do they like to talk about all the time? Do they give you good counsel or have they misled you several times as a leader or aspiring leader? Be wise for evil communication corrupt good manners. Young man, young woman, old boys and girls; be wise hence you make yourself a prey to END your better tomorrow and days for friends. A genuine leader will make those around him/her feel respected and valued.

God's blessings will never elude you as you keep still to reading this piece of material as a soon to be or already existing leader. Make leader's anchor a daily anchor for your desired success and lift in leadership.

Impactor Victor Elendu

REVIEWS:

Mr. Ntegun, Emmanuel Lawson: "great stride/bold step in the right direction towards the training of great minds for nations building.

CONTACT THE AUTHOR:

FACEBOOK: Impactor Victor Elendu

Email: IVEbooks@hotmail.com

PHONE NUMBERS: 08051886143, 08066527613

ABOUT THE AUTHOR

Driven with the passion to restore hope to humanity, Impactor Victor Elendu accepted his call into the evangelical ministry from teenage and has been pursuing it fervently till this time.

As a student in River State College of Health Science and Technology Port Harcourt; He served in Christ Ambassador Student Outreach (CASOR) as; President, General Secretary, and Prayer Secretary.

His love for God and Humanity led him to begin a foundation, known as Fix the Youth Initiative with the aim of reaching out youth. This foundation was birthed during his National Youth Service Corp at Eastern part of Nigeria.

He is an uncommon Leader, currently serving in God's Covenant Children Outreach as the Missions Coordinator.

He is life coach, mentor and many passionate and purpose driven youth of our time.

www.ingramcontent.com/pod-product-compliance
Lightning Source LLC
Chambersburg PA
CBHW052118150726
48002CB00006B/2394